Small Talk

Nic Aubury

Nasty Little Press

Published by Nasty Little Press in December 2011.
Reprinted in 2012 (3)

Nasty Little Press
35 St Johns Road, Bungay, Suffolk

nastylittlepress.org

Printed and bound by Beforts Information Press Ltd.
23-25 Gunnels Wood Park, Gunnels Wood Road, Stevenage, Herts

ISBN: 978-0-9563767-9-4

Nasty Little Press is the proud recipient of a Grants for the Arts
Award from Arts Council England.

LOTTERY FUNDED

for Tom, Jamie and Fred

Acknowledgements

Special thanks to Luke Wright and Sally Roe at Nasty Little Press.

Sincere thanks also to Emma Aubury for her patience and support, and to Ben Raudnitz and Daviona Watt for their advice and encouragement.

Contents

The New Year

To a raucous, plastic fanfare
at midnight she arrives.
By way of greeting, slurring husbands
argue with their wives.

Stillettoed girls - mascara-streaked
and wearing borrowed coats -
stand shivering, whilst hair-gelled boys
still hope to get their oats.

Her way is strewn with lager cans
the debris from kebabs
and the contents of the ashtrays
of a row of mini-cabs.

It really isn't hard to see
how she might take offence
and why she spends the next twelve months
demanding recompense.

Magpie Smallprint

One for sorrow
Two for joy
Three for a girl
Four for a boy
Five for silver
Six for gold
Seven for a secret never to be told*

*Just how close in time and space do magpies need to be
for them to count on aggregate and not just separately?
If today I saw one magpie, then another one tomorrow,
would that be two for joy, or two separate lots of sorrow?
And what if you get eight or more at once? It may be rare,
but is the whole thing then just void? That doesn't seem quite fair.
And can you split them into groups? If I saw seven, say,
then I'd rather joy plus silver than a secret any day.
With stuff like joy and sorrow the distinction is important,
and as things stand we might expect an outcome which we oughtn't.
For matters of such magnitude (or magpitude?) it's right
that there shouldn't be grey areas: it should be black and white.

No Strings

Gentlemen of any age,
observe this rule of thumb:
it's hard to make an entrance
when you're dropped off by your mum.

Ambition / Ambitioff

Here's to mediocrity,
to pottering and making tea,
to comfortable and muddling through,
to 'not too bad' and 'that'll do'.

Good luck to those who chase a goal
and scrabble up the greasy pole
and push themselves to be the best -
but I'll take poor and not so stressed.

The Sommelier and Some Liar

Knowledgeable-nonchalant,
I tell the waiter 'Fine'
when really what I'm thinking is
'I'm fairly sure it's wine.'

Unfairy Tale

I wish I could console you with the hope of happy endings
or of swift poetic justice, or unlikely strokes of luck.
I fear, though, that the truth is, if you're born an ugly duckling,
then there's every chance, in time, that you'll become an ugly duck.

Reflections on a French Holiday

Sandy towels.
Gallic scowls.
Upset bowels.

Let's Call the Whole Thing Odd

I say 'suave' and you say 'state';
I say 'digit', you say 'eight';
I say 'soak' and you say 'rock';
I say 'coal' and you say 'cock';
I say 'stop' and you say 'rump';
I say 'runs' and you say 'pump';
I say 'jazz' and you say 'lazy';
I say 'fairy', you say 'daisy'.
I say 'bald', and you say 'cake';
I say 'calf', and you say 'bake';
I was at first a bit perplexed;
I've now switched off predictive text.

RSVP

It seems that you like me enough that you'd ask me
to buy you a coffee machine,
or a wall-mounted clock, or a new iPod dock,
or a Villeroy and Boch figurine;
enough that you'd ask for a Waterford vase
or a full set of white, cotton bedding,
but not quite enough that you'd actually like me
to come to the whole of your wedding.

Bridging the Gap

I can't recall the moment when
I thought that I'd look better
in some Marks & Spencer trousers
and a v-necked lambswool sweater
and I know for sure it wasn't
a deliberate decision
to become a man who falls asleep
whilst watching television
and who always has a handkerchief
and listens to the news
and who gardens at the weekends
and who polishes his shoes.

Your parents' great revenge, it seems,
for all you put them through
is that, without your noticing,
you end up more like them than you.

Special Relationship

America's all *Dog eat dog*
and *Flaunt 'em if you've got 'em;*
an English dog's more likely just
to sniff another's bottom.

Cockney Rhyming Limerick

There was an old man from Quebec
Who had a peculiar *Gregory*.
A passing giraffe
Said: 'You're having a *Steffi*:
That's one for the doctor to *Ant*!'

Small Talk

It fails to impress you,
when you mention Mogadishu,
that I reply with 'Bless you',
and offer you a tissue.

Feedback

Thanks for coming William -
we're grateful for your time.
Well, we read the group your poem,
and it mostly went down fine.
Of course, some lines they didn't like -
that's really nothing strange -
and we'd like to talk you through the parts
we'd recommend you change.

They felt the talk of 'loneliness'
and 'clouds' was quite depressing
and for your older readership
potentially distressing.
They thought it would be nicer,
when going for your walk,
if you'd chosen sunny weather
and a friend with whom to talk.

To some the rural setting
of the vales and hills was sweet,
but many found it 'out of touch' -
they'd rather see a street.
Now, if you think an urban scene
would make things feel too stark,
we're sure a compromise could work -
a garden, or a park?

But here's the really tricky bit -
we've workshopped it for hours -
they really weren't too sure at all
about your choice of flowers.
The thing that they objected to -
and bear in mind your sales -
is that daffodils remind them all
so dreadfully of Wales.

The Beautiful Game

To men, it's far more than just twenty-two people
running and kicking a ball:
it's something to talk to each other about
whilst still saying nothing at all.

X and Y

Inside the latest *Marie Claire*
they've got an eight page questionnaire
to help you judge if you and he
are really, truly meant to be;
to help you tell if, on reflection,
there's a spiritual connection
of the sort there needs to be
for amatory harmony.

In *FHM* this month they've gone
for Kelly Brook without much on.

Those Who Can't

The teacher liked the desks to be
in neat and tidy rows.
That's why the sad git ended up
a teacher, I suppose.

Round the Bend

Outside the car, my father-in-law -
all pantomime gestures and strange semaphore -
is directing me into a large parking space
with pompous concern etched into his face.
Right hand down now! he suddenly yelps,
seeming to think that this actually helps;
reversing, I'm tempted to see if he feels
so inclined to advise me from under my wheels.

The First Mrs. Spratt

Jack's first wife would give him strife
when served with her main course:
'I'll not eat that - it's all just fat!'
It ended in divorce.

If Sweden were Swindon

If Sweden were Swindon
we wouldn't have Ikea,
or Tetra Pak, or Volvo cars,
or Saab, or *Mamma Mia!*
We'd still be using Fahrenheit
we'd have no Nobel prizes
but Stockholm and its roundabouts
would be quite near Devizes.

Dead Set

A subject to which I've devoted some thought is
the posture I'd choose for my own *rigor mortis*;
whatever position my heirs see me off in,
I hope it requires a custom-built coffin.

No Kids, Please

Some don't pass the parcel on
but hold it 'til the music stops;
in time, they'll find out if they've won
or if it's just an empty box.

Candlelight

The poet's life would be far sweeter
were there money in the metre.

Growing Pains
for Jamie, Aged 5

In time, I know, I'll irritate,
you'll slam your door, profess to hate
and it will all be *so* unfair -
I could die, for all you'll care.

But as you now fold into me
with tear-streaked face and bloodied knee
what's important stays unspoken
and, what's more, cannot be broken.

The Punchline

'Knock knock' began the boy, and so 'Who's there?' obliged his dad,
and then, trying not to giggle yet, 'I dunnap' said the lad.
'I dunnap who?' the dad said; 'YOU DONE A POO!' the boy,
as gleeful as an unspoiled child unwrapping his first toy.
He didn't see the irony, though, when, by happenstance,
he laughed so much he lost control and soiled his underpants.

A Problem Shared is a Problem Doubled

When you woke me to tell me that you couldn't sleep
what did you hope I could do?
Was there simply some comfort, as you tossed and turned,
in seeing me suffering too?
With a groan you declared that with less than eight hours
it starts to impinge on your health,
but it seems it was fine to impose upon me
what you couldn't endure for yourself.
Now, as before, one of us is awake;
my resentment is starting to grow.
It's clear that I won't fall asleep for a while
and I'm thinking of letting you know.

Emoticon

Semi-colon, right-hand bracket.
Smiley face? I'd like to smack it. ;)

Whatever Happened to Peter and Jane?

Here is Peter. Here is Jane.
How nice to see them both again!
You last met in the seventies
when they were both in dungarees.

Now they've grown up, just like you,
with mortgages and pensions too.
Peter's working in I.T.
and Jane's what's called a 'divorcee'.

Look - can you see Peter's pill?
He worked too hard, and then got ill.
And can you see Jane's Chardonnay?
She drinks a bottle every day!

They've moved away from their home town.
She used to phone when she felt down.
They hardly see each other now.
Their parents died. They had a row.

Remember how they used to play
Through one, unending summer's day?
Where *has* the time gone? Do you know?
It seems so very long ago.

Just Write

These days there are workshops and courses and so on
for people who wish to be writers to go on.
However, I'd happily bet a few quid
that Byron and Shelley and Keats never did.

Ever After

A happy ending isn't an ending -
it's stopping the story half-way through.
An ending is moving away, or divorce,
or you mourning her, or her mourning you.

Also by NASTY LITTLE PRESS

High Performance
by Luke Wright
ISBN: 978-0-9563767-0-1 | £5

The Vile Ascent Of Lucien Gore And What The People Did
by Luke Wright
ISBN: 978-0-9563767-2-5 | £5

Boring The Arse Off Young People
by Martin Figura
ISBN: 978-0-9563767-3-2 | £5

Under The Pier
by Salena Godden
ISBN: 978-0-9563767-4-9 | £5

Whenever I Get Blown Up I Think Of You
by Molly Naylor
ISBN: 978-0-9563767-5-6 | £10

The New Blur Album
by John Osborne
ISBN: 978-0-9563767-7-0 | £5

www.nastylittlepress.org